What Should We Be Teaching in the Social Studies?

by
Richard E. Gross
and
Thomas L. Dynneson

Library of Congress Catalog Card Number 83-61786
ISBN 0-87367-199-6
Copyright © 1983 by the Phi Delta Kappa Educational Foundation
Bloomington, Indiana

This fastback is sponsored by the Fort Hays State University Chapter of Phi Delta Kappa in Hays, Kansas, which made a generous contribution toward publication costs.

The chapter sponsors this fastback in memory of Dr. Jimmy Rice, fellow Kappan, longtime membership vice president of the chapter, and dean of the Fort Hays University Graduate School.

Table of Contents

Table of Contents

Foreword

The publication of this fastback on social studies curriculum revision is timely. Public concern for improving education is high; and it is widely recognized that citizens of the twenty-first century will face more complex environmental, economic, and social problems than ever before. It is also clear that in order to prepare youth adequately for the future, citizenship education must be revised and revitalized now.

The National Council for the Social Studies (NCSS) will soon publish a report on scope and sequence that offers guidance to school systems undertaking curriculum revision and recommends ways to modify the traditional program to prepare students for an increasingly interdependent world. This fastback is an important complement to the NCSS scope and sequence project. It provides historical background on how the social studies curriculum evolved and describes the forces that influence curriculum change. To paraphrase Santayana, history repeats itself only when we fail to learn the lessons of the past. Through this publication, Professors Gross and Dynneson may save us from that fate.

We are grateful to James A. Banks, past president of NCSS, who initiated this cooperative publishing project between NCSS and Phi Delta Kappa. And we appreciate the efforts of Derek L. Burleson, editor of Special Publications at Phi Delta Kappa, who supported the idea and carried it through to reality. Finally, we want to thank Richard Gross and Thomas Dynneson for their research, reflections, and advice. It is now up to us to meet the difficult — and very important — challenge of redesigning citizenship education to meet the needs of a rapidly changing world.

Carole L. Hahn, President
National Council for the
Social Studies, 1983

Where Are We Today?

Assessing the current status of the social studies curriculum is no easy task. The hectic developments of the late Sixties and early Seventies, which included the era of the "new social studies," resulted in a condition resembling curricular anarchy. But to what extent did these new programs and approaches find their way into an established scope and sequence? Have the schools turned back to traditional social studies?

For a number of years some social studies education leaders have felt the need to assess the status and the direction of the social studies. A recent effort was in the summer of 1982, when a group of social studies educators met in Wisconsin at the Wingspread Conference Center to "rethink" the social studies. This far too short, three-day conference attempted to identify some possible directions for revitalizing the social studies in light of the perceived problems that plague the profession. The participants left the conference with a new awareness of the issues and with an increased recognition of the challenges of current diversity, multiple prescriptions and remedies, declining curricular influence, and an almost powerless leadership that now characterize our field. Unfortunately, the several working parties did not have time to reach a consensus on national directions for the social studies.[1]

In recent years hundreds of recommendations for change have been made, thousands of pages describing "innovative" models and programs have been written, and millions of dollars have been spent on revisions. The results are less than encouraging. One could conclude that we are almost helpless in terms of bringing about real and lasting change at the state and local levels, or of reaching some national consensus about the social studies curriculum. If we as a profession have failed to bring about change, we reasonably might ask how programs can be changed and stabilized and by whom.

On a national level, patterns that do exist seem to be maintained primarily by tradition and by the influence of major textbook companies whose textbooks continue to mimic one another, holding to established patterns rather than striking out in new directions. A historical review of the social studies field indicates that new models and proposals are likely to be ignored by the majority of classroom teachers. Few proposals ever achieved large-scale implementation. As a profession, we have failed to agree on the direction of change and have failed to prepare the way for constructive change. As a result, we have an over-burdened, ill-defined, and fractured field limping haltingly into an era that demands civic involvement, social responsibility, economic competency, and historical grounding on a local, national, and international scale.

A Comparison of Two Studies
on the Status of the Social Studies

In 1977 Richard E. Gross published the results of a study that he had conducted nationally on the status of the social studies. Among his findings were:

- There is no standardized social studies program within many states, let alone throughout the country.
- U.S. history and government courses have held their enrollments, while enrollments in other standard social studies courses have tended to lose ground.
- Secondary school administrators tended to be more supportive of social studies than elementary principals, but the social studies as a curriculum area have lost ground within the general school program.
- School districts in the 1970s were cutting back on social studies curriculum material purchases.
- Elementary social studies are the weakest aspect of the social studies curriculum.
- The 1916 secondary social studies curriculum pattern established by the NEA Commission on the Reorganization of Secondary Education had been "shattered" by recent events. These events included policy changes with regard to course requirements and the advent of the "new social studies."[2]

9

The most startling claim in the Gross study was the conclusion that the 1916 curriculum pattern seemed to have been "shattered." This general pattern had been extremely durable, especially at the high school level, and provided some standardization for the nation's social studies course offerings for over 60 years.

Subsequently, a second study on the status of the social studies curriculum was published in 1982 by researchers at the Social Science Education Consortium in Boulder, Colorado. Their findings did not support all of Gross' conclusions about the status of the social studies. According to them, the social studies curriculum exhibited the following characteristics:

There is great uniformity within the social studies. This uniformity is expressed in a standardization within the following K-12 curriculum pattern:

Kindergarten — self, school, community, home
Grade 1 — Families
Grade 2 — Neighbors
Grade 3 — Communities
Grade 4 — State history
Grade 5 — U.S. history
Grade 6 — World cultures
Grade 7 — World geography or history
Grade 8 — American history
Grade 9 — Civics or world cultures
Grade 10 — World history
Grade 11 — American history
Grade 12 — American government

For secondary schools the pattern of courses recommended by the 1916 NEA Commission on the Reorganization of Secondary Schools was still in place.

Commercial social studies textbooks are the dominant instrument of instruction in the social studies.

The commercial social studies textbook has been modified somewhat in recent years by being more "pluralistic," being less nationalistic, being more world dependency oriented, emphasizing a greater number of teaching methodologies, and containing some ideas that originated with the "new social studies."[3]

While the Colorado group conducted its study later and expanded its focus into more areas than the ones reported by Gross, the point of contention between these two studies was the degree of standardization that exists within the social studies curriculum. Perhaps these differences can be explained by the nature of the two investigations. While Gross used data reported on questionnaires from school personnel, the Colorado study used course titles and scope and sequence charts found in district curriculum guides and state reports. Course titles tend to report on the general framework of the social studies curriculum without giving much detailed information on the specifics of the course. Also, two teachers teaching from the same framework can vary the emphasis of their instruction so much that there is little similarity between what takes place in one classroom and another classroom. Frameworks and scope and sequence charts are poor predictors of the actual practices of teachers. While these lead some researchers to report standardization within the curriculum, a closer look may well reveal that such seeming likeness is a myth. The myth of standardization is perpetuated by the assumption that teachers actually follow and teach from curriculum guidelines and state frameworks. More often than not, they teach from highly structured textbooks, which include some of the features of these frameworks; but they may actually be teaching a variety of courses under the same course title. A more accurate picture of the status of the social studies may be found in a careful examination of social studies textbooks and, particularly, of the behaviors of individual teachers. The patterns of textbook adoptions, as well as the content of local and state-administered tests, also may help to reveal the degree of standardization that actually exists in the curriculum.

"Where are we today?" is a question that is difficult to assess, but it is a fundamental question that must be answered if we are to move on to specific recommendations regarding the future of the social studies curriculum. At present, it seems that we are in a kind of "no man's land," unsure of where we are and unsure of our next move. If this is the current condition within the social studies, what then can we reasonably

11

conclude about the status of the social studies? We might conclude the following:

- We do not know definitely where the social studies curriculum stands in terms of standardization and in terms of its importance to the schools.
- There is no identifiable trend or direction that points the way to the future of the social studies.
- Social studies leaders are not in agreement about what should be done, although they are willing to talk and to disagree. But can they find a consensus?
- Social studies teachers are not easily influenced by individuals or leaders within the profession.
- In order to control the grassroots level of instruction, commercial textbook publishers must be willing to cooperate with those who seek change.
- Current social, political, and economic factors must be assessed in order to give effective direction to the future of the social studies curriculum.
- The general trends and directions within education also will influence the future direction of the social studies.

Problems and Issues Currently Confronting the Social Studies

In 1979 Gross and Dynneson identified eight fundamental questions pertaining to the future of the social studies curriculum:

1. What should be the basis for selection of content in the social studies?
2. Can we identify the most efficient scope and sequence for the social studies curriculum?
3. Should there be a "common core" of shared social studies throughout the elementary and secondary curriculum?
4. What position should the social studies take on achievement tests?
5. How can teachers change and how can improvements be achieved in the social studies?
6. What means are available to ensure improved implementation of new courses, approaches, and materials in the social studies?
7. How can the impact of elementary social studies be extended?
8. How can the status of the social studies be improved?

During the summer of 1979, more than 50 social studies leaders attempted to answer these questions and to provide recommendations to the profession. Some of the results of this National Science Foundation conference at Stanford University were published in the May 1980 issue of *Social Education*.[4] These same questions need to be asked throughout the nation in order to stimulate dialogue, which could lead to a "new consensus" among social studies educators.

13

In the fall of 1980, educators associated with the SPAN Project located at Boulder, Colorado, identified six important problems that currently plague the social studies:

1. Student Learning: Too many students fail to learn important social studies knowledge, skills, and attitudes and do not like or value social studies.

2. Teacher Instruction: Instruction in social studies is generally characterized by lack of variety in teaching methods and evaluation practices, limited kinds of learning experiences, and inattention to the implications of educational research.

3. Curriculum: The present social studies curriculum does not contribute as much as it could to learning that is useful for helping students understand and participate more effectively in the current and future social world.

4. Profession: The social studies profession is characterized by a lack of constructive interaction among various participants, by limited opportunities for professional growth for teachers, and by confusion about the role of social studies in the education of young people.

5. Culture of School: The culture and organization of the school focus much of the energy of teachers and administrators on matters of management and control rather than on teaching and learning.

6. Public Awareness: The public does not fully understand or appreciate the importance of social studies.

These problems identified by the SPAN associates served as a basis for reexamining the current condition of the social studies curriculum. The end product of this effort was the development of a K-12 social studies curriculum that focused on the social roles of individuals living in American society.[5] However, support in practice of these recommendations has been minimal at best, as far as the writers of this fastback have been able to discern.

In addition to the above current issues, many problems have long haunted the social studies curriculum. Some years ago, Richard E.

Gross and Dwight Allen identified two important issues that have affected the social studies curriculum for more than 60 years. These issues center on the teacher's ability and willingness 1) to execute instruction according to the most "appropriate organizational framework" for the social studies and 2) to handle the essential and updated content of their field.[6] These two issues persist because of the continuing turnover of teachers, the additive nature of knowledge, and the need to adjust the curriculum framework to accommodate emerging instructional programs.

Today the public as well as many professionals seek an end to the near-anarchy that has beset our field. The back-to-basics movement has brought a decline of mini-courses, electives, and of social studies requirements. Creativity and innovation are no longer the "in" words in education. There is a growing call for excellence in learning and educational accountability. It would seem to be an ideal time to press for stabilization in the social studies.

New directions should emerge from social studies leadership at the state and national levels. Without leadership at these levels, the profession will drift along in an aimless state that could lead to even more chaotic conditions. National leadership can bring order out of chaos by coordinating the effort to identify prime societal factors and public demands, to reassess conditions within the curriculum, and to provide the framework and direction that is necessary to give meaning and revived importance to our social studies programs. Unless this is accomplished, the current chaotic conditions within the social studies profession and within the curriculum undoubtedly will continue.

The Historical Roots of the
Social Studies Curriculum

In asking the question, "Where are we today?" it is also useful to ask, "Where have we been?" Tracing the roots of the social studies curriculum gives a sense of the growth and development that has occurred. One of the conclusions that probably would emerge from such a study is that the social studies curriculum is directly influenced by the social and intellectual events that have occurred in American society. Thus, if responsive, the social studies curriculum should reflect the beliefs, events, and conditions that were and are important to society as a whole.

Social Education Prior to the Civil War

Education in colonial America can be equated with religious education. If a colonial social studies curriculum could be identified, it probably would consist of the rudiments of geography, Biblical history, and some aspects of European backgrounds and of colonial history. Christian ethics could be equated with a type of values education that attempted to teach students the "golden rule," which related to behavior and conduct within the Christian lifestyle. The purpose of citizenship education was to promote church membership.[7] Ethics, virtues, ideals, and attitudes helped to shape the conduct of the individual both in his private and public life.

The American Revolution led to a shift from colonial institutions to the emergence of new national institutions whose philosophic roots were embedded in the Age of Enlightenment. Secularism would in time replace the religious institutions that were dominant in American education. These new institutions would focus on the establishment of a

16

democratic republican form of rule and the education of the common man so that he could participate in the new society. As education historian Freeman R. Butts put it:

> [T]he welfare of the Republic rested upon an educated citizenry and that republican schools — especially free, common, public schools — would be the best means of educating citizenry in the civic values, knowledge, and obligations required of everyone in a democratic republican society.[8]

Public education would take more than a century to evolve into a structure recognizable today. In the meantime, the attention of the new republic would focus on more practical matters such as the settling of the great frontier. However, from 1795 to the 1850s, social studies textbooks were written for school children, dealing primarily with geography, history, and civics. Before the Civil War, geography was the dominant content area in the social studies. Most of it was oriented toward the elementary school. Secondary education as a public institution would not emerge as an important element until after the 1880s.

Social Education After the Civil War — 1865 to 1880

The Civil War was a major turning point for the United States in terms of the changes that would occur and the effects that these changes would have on the nation's institutions. The Industrial Revolution would bring changes related to the rapid development of urban and industrial life. Shifts in population and immigration created new needs and some severe problems that would affect public education. After the Civil War, history replaced geography as the dominant discipline in the social studies, because it was believed that a study of history would help the nation by socializing citizens from various cultural backgrounds who had migrated to the United States. The history of that era, as reflected in standard history textbooks, was a special kind of history. It was a patriotic history based on an emotional plea aimed at winning the loyalty of the common man to the ideals of the American dream. It was a nationalistic history wrapped in Americanism. For example, American heroes were not ordinary men but men of great virtue and unusual ability, who were given opportunities that were not available in other lands.

Historian George Bancroft had exerted considerable influence in producing public school history textbooks with a patriotic emphasis.

> To the resplendent values of liberty, equality, patriotism, and benevolent Christian morality were now added the middle-class virtues of hard work, honesty and integrity, the rewards of individual effort, and obedience to legitimate authority.[9]

History was made into a sort of discipline with a special task: "[I]t served as moral and religious training, it offered training in citizenship and inspired patriotism."[10]

Meanwhile, university scholars toward the end of the 19th century had moved in the direction of a more objective or "scientific" history. They were not satisfied with the nationalistic approach and protested the way that it was presented to students in the public schools. They also felt that this type of history was a threat to the very concept of democratic citizenship in which the individual was expected to consider issues, weigh outcomes, make decisions, and participate in the debates of the great issues of their times.

Social Education in the Age of Reform — 1880 to 1910

The Industrial Revolution and its accompanying effects on urbanism and immigration led to many social ills, which in turn led to the need for social reform. During this same period, secondary education began to emerge as the public schools expanded. Institutions of higher learning also were emerging as part of public education. An important question regarding the high school curriculum was whether the high school was to prepare students for higher education or was it to be a terminal institution for the vast numbers of students who would attend it.

At this time new professional societies were being organized to serve both scholars and teachers. The National Education Association (NEA) was organized after the Civil War. The American Historical Association (AHA) was founded in 1884. Historians were concerned with the teaching of history at both the pre-collegiate and collegiate levels, particularly the type of history that was being taught in the public schools. Between 1880 and 1890 university academicians attempted to replace this nationalistic history with a more scientific history. They wanted to supplement the textbook with primary sources in order to give a more balanced perspective.[11]

During this period the curriculum was becoming more standardized through the growing influence of state education agencies and the standardization of textbooks.[12] Social reform reflected in the rise of organized labor was also being felt in education. State legislatures passed child labor laws and expanded their support for public education. The progressive movement took hold in this period and became a major force in American life in the decades ahead. These influences would directly affect curriculum development, especially in the social studies.

The Influence of National Committees — 1894 to 1934

While control of the schools is a local and state function, a national curriculum began to emerge in the 1890s as a result of the work of various national committees appointed by education and academic associations. These committees usually were given specific problems to resolve, but in some cases they went well beyond their assigned tasks and dealt with issues that were of more concern to them. These committees produced influential reports and recommendations at a time when the teacher looked to outside authority for direction. It was a time when academic figures in higher education had a great influence on the curriculum. In essence, classroom teachers were being told what should be studied and how one should learn.[13]

The committees that influenced the social studies curriculum included the following:

1893 — The NEA Committee of Ten was concerned with the general high school curriculum and whether it should be designed as a terminal education or as preparation for college. The final committee report recommended that the curriculum include strong academic courses for the non-college bound majority of students. History was to emphasize a scientific approach rather than a patriotic approach.[14]

1899 — The AHA Committee of Seven, made up of eminent historians, was concerned about the teaching of history in the public schools. It recommended a dominant position for history in the curriculum,[15] with an emphasis on the use of primary sources and historical inquiry in order to encourage high school students to weigh evidence, draw conclusions, and conduct historical research.[16]

1905 — The AHA Committee of Eight was concerned with the teaching of history in the elementary school. Its report recommended that Old World history be added to the sixth grade as a background for American history taught in higher grades.

1916 — The NEA Commission on the Reorganization of Secondary Education was charged with studying the entire secondary curriculum, including all areas of the social studies. The term "social studies" began to be used officially at this time to designate the disciplines of history and related areas. The progressive movement was running at high tide during this period and many of the educators that served on the various committees of the NEA Commission were supporters of progressive principles.

Between 1900 and 1916, the work of historian James Harvey Robinson was influencing historians. His approach, called "new history," was rooted in "social efficiency" and "social history" rather than political history. Robinson's approach, when combined with the pedagogical principles of Dewey, changed the direction of the social studies from "scientific history" to citizenship and social efficiency.[17] As a result of these and other influences, the commission's committee on the social studies recommended that the primary role of the social studies was to develop effective citizenship. Arthur W. Dunn, who served on the commission, had written *The Community and the Citizen* in 1907, in which he recommended that the social studies be expanded to include more areas and disciplines than just history. His approach to the social studies also focused on citizenship.[18]

The recommendations of the commission included a scope and sequence for secondary social studies, which became the dominant pattern for secondary schools for more than 60 years; and its influence is still substantial. The sequence was as follows:

Grade 7 — European history and geography
Grade 8 — American history
Grade 9 — Civics

Grade 10 — European history
Grade 11 — American history
Grade 12 — Government or problems of democracy

1918 — The Final Report of the NEA Commission on the Reorganization of Secondary Education contained the now well-known Seven Cardinal Principles of Education, which influenced general education as well as the social studies. These seven principles served as criteria that could help guide the development of programs and were used as the basis for the new comprehensive high school curriculum.[19] The Seven Cardinal Principles are:

Health
Command of fundamental processes
Worthy home membership
Vocation
Citizenship
Worthy use of leisure
Ethical character

While citizenship was included as a general educational principle, its implementation fell primarily in the social studies area.[20]

1929 — The American Historical Association, during the 1920s, continued to be interested in the way history was being taught in the public schools. In 1926 the AHA Committee on History and the Social Studies reported that the curriculum programs in the schools were "candidly moribund." The chairman, August C. Krey, recommended a five-year study that would lead to the revitalization of history.[21] As a result of this recommendation, in 1929 the AHA authorized the establishment of the Commission on the Social Studies, which was supported by a grant from the Carnegie Corporation.

During the depression years of the 1930s, some historians began to view American institutions from the perspective of "social reconstructionism," which was a synthesis of older progressive ideas and "New Deal" politics. Such like-minded men as George S. Counts, John Dewey, John L. Childs, William H. Kilpatrick, Jesse Newlon, Harold Rugg, and Merle Curti contributed heavily to this perspective and influenced the commission.[22] The social reconstructionists believed that laissez-faire approaches to economics and government had run their course and that the times called for planning and regulatory measures in order to cure the social ills brought on by industrialization and urbanization.[23]

The work of the commission resulted in 17 volumes, the last of which included "Conclusions and Recommendations." Charles A. Beard, the eminent historian, played a major role in the development, writing, and editing of these reports. The reports were fairly well received by social studies teachers and they did have some influence. However, they attempted to displace citizenship as the focus of the social studies with a scholarly type of history and social science.[24] This shift did not take place, and citizenship remained as the accepted charge of the social studies.

The commission members met at Princeton, N.J., in 1933 to adopt the "Conclusions and Recommendations," but they did not succeed because of the differences that arose between the liberal and conservative members on the commission. As a result, the AHA ended the work of the commission in 1934 and no new national curriculum pattern emerged.[25]

Scope and Sequence Recommendations of Selected Social Studies Leaders

No historical overview of the social studies field would be complete without acknowledging the contributions of some of the leaders in the field. The 1920s and 1930s was a period of increasing activity in social studies curriculum development. During these years leaders in the emerging social studies profession were proposing a variety of approaches to the social studies curriculum. In 1939 the NCSS issued the first of a series of curriculum publications titled, *The Future of the Social Studies*. It was edited by James A. Michener, who was later to become one of our most prolific and popular writers of historical fiction.

Michener invited the leading social studies educators of the day to write articles describing alternative approaches and designs for a social studies curriculum. The publication contained 15 articles on curriculum design in the social studies. While few of these curricula were ever adopted on a wide scale, they provoked others to think of alternative directions for the social studies. Remember that this was a period when there were few sources of funds for curriculum experimentation. Six of the curricula are summarized here. Included with each approach are a rationale and a scope and sequence of course offerings for each grade level.

The Community or Civic-Centered Approach. During the 1930s the community-centered curriculum was popular among some social studies educators. The goals of this approach included skills related to personal needs of the child. In addition, cooperative group skills, participation in community affairs, the development of social values, and knowledge of current events were emphasized. Mary G. Kelty was a leading advocate of this approach. She proposed an intriguing curriculum for the social studies arising from two major sources:

> . . . the world of nature and of man — to which converge and with which are integrated many branches from other directions. The social science trunk system will consist of four main lines, complementary in their nature, running throughout the school experience. These are: 1) the management by the group of its own affairs, largely in connection with 2 and 3 [below]; 2) the working with adults on community projects of civic concern; 3) as a major center, a developmental sequence planned to secure growth in desirable direction through materials chosen for social value, scholarship value, and contribution of child growth; 4) the reading of current events.[26]

She proposed the following scope and sequence:

Grade	Subject
K	The world of the child
1 — 3	Emphasis on student participation:
	a. affairs of the classroom
	b. affairs of the community
	c. affairs of the home
	d. affairs of the school

4 — 5	Emphasis on group interaction:
	a. work and participation with adults
	b. the child and social values
	c. the issues and problems of society
6 — 8	The national scene: world civilization and modern cultures including current history
9	An intensive study of the local community
10 — 12	A mixture of subjects and concerns:

           a. how different communities handle local situations

           b. cooperative projects between students and the community

           c. current events

           d. human relations

           e. homemaking

           (11th grade would concentrate on the study of American history)

The Social Problems Approach. This approach attempted to prepare students to deal with the present and future problems of their society. It is based, in part, on the premise that students can learn those problem-solving processes needed to cope with complex social problems. Samuel P. McCutchen is the educator most closely associated with this approach to the social studies. His rationale is best stated in his own words:

> If we can no longer teach students all that they will need to know in later life, neither can we predict with any accuracy the social, economic, or political problems with which they will be confronted in later years. It should be possible, however, to teach students a way of facing social problems and to give them such practice in using a specific process on problems of concern to them now, that the scientific way of approaching problems will become a habit.[27]
> . . . [I]f we wish to develop in students the ability to face social problems scientifically, it seems to follow that they must be confronted regularly and frequently with social problems which are real to them, and that they be assisted in each problem to a definite process of scientific thinking[28]

McCutchen's suggested scope and sequence for grades 7 through 12 included a problems approach using units that focus on personal-social problems, community problems, contemporary problems, and applied problems as an aspect of history. In grades 11 and 12 there would be an emphasis on survey courses including world history, American history, and contemporary society.[29]

The World Approach. This approach, emphasizing both national and world affairs, is associated with Frances Morehouse, who was concerned with the rebuilding of American institutions through an improved educational system. She was also interested in better education for the average and brighter students, which may have been her reaction to the child-centered approaches that were popular at the time. Her rationale was that content should be:

> . . . arranged in sequence of increased difficulty, of appropriate interests for each grade, of progressing from familiar and concrete things to unfamiliar and generalized knowledge, all intended not to center the pupils' attention on their own lives and interests, but on the nature, needs, and possibilities of the world about them.[30]

She proposed the following scope and sequence:

Grade	Subject
1	My family and my school
2	My community
3	The lives of children far away
4	The lives of grown-ups whom the world cannot forget
5	Functional geography of the United States
6	Functional geography of the world
7	United States history to 1865
8	United States history from 1865 to the present
9	Ancient and medieval history to the invention of printing
10	Modern Old World history from 1450 to the present
11	New World histroy
12	Economics and political sciences[31]

The Social Reconstructionist Approach. This approach emphasized the reform of American social institutions. Social reconstructionism was popular in the 1930s because of the problems associated with the Great Depression. Many became convinced that social reform could be achieved through institutional regulations and "scientifically" planned programs. According to this approach, the schools would become the agent for building a new society. Harold Rugg is the educator associated with this approach. He spent a lifetime attempting to develop a curriculum that would help change American society. This curriculum would focus on what Rugg called the "American Problem": "I have tried many leads but none has been so helpful to my own practice as the vision of millions of young Americans working at the American Problem."[32]

While Rugg failed to bring about the changes that he had envisioned, his commitment to social change through educational means is a different and interesting view regarding the relationship between the curriculum and American society. Before his career came to an end, Rugg became a controversial educator. Critics charged that his views were anti-capitalistic and un-American.

According to Rugg's rationale:

> The new school . . . is the potentially powerful leader in the study of society. Among its other objectives, it is committed to turning out youth who do understand American life as it is actually lived, who are deeply concerned to help build a decent civilization on our continent and are convinced that it can be done.[33]

He proposed the following scope and sequence:

Grade	Subject (Each topic usually for one-half year).
K – 2	No recommendation
3	Earth, universe, and nature (primitive) peoples
4	Communities of men and peoples and countries
5	The building of America and man at work
6	Man at work: His arts and crafts and mankind developing civilization throughout the ages
7	Introduction to the study of American civilization and Europe builds industrial civilization and Europeanizes the Earth

26

8	The history in back of the American Problem: Land conquest and development and the beginnings of a unique democracy
9	Community and national life and the rebuilding of America
10	World problems and world history
11 — 12	The American Problem and its historical background[34]

The Child-Centered or Individualized Approach. This approach focused on the needs of the individual child. It is based on the assumption that the curriculum cannot be dictated or prescribed prior to assessing the needs of the child. Promoted by Donnal V. Smith as an alternative to existing programs in the social studies, his rationale was that:

> If public education is to aid the development of each individual's powers and abilities in this direction, it must always concern itself with the individual. . . .
>
> The social-education program must accept the psychological premise that the child learns those things which coincide with and are an outgrowth of, or a development from, his own experiences and are directly related to his own welfare. The social-studies program must be one which establishes satisfaction for the learner; one which will measure its progress entirely in terms of the development of the particular individual.[35]

His proposed scope and sequence is as follows:

Grade	Subject
K — 2	General education
3 — 4	The world of the child and community: analysis of the larger community
5	The nation
6	East-West relationships: National groups and cultures
7 — 12	The secondary curriculum focuses on the students'

individualized growth and development with three major emphases:

a. Social organization
b. The evolution of social organizations
c. The issues of living in modern cultures

The Good Citizenship Approach. Traditionally, a major responsibility of the social studies has been preparation of "good" citizens. This approach emphasizes the values, skills, and content that grew out of our democratic traditions and institutions. Howard E. Wilson is associated with this approach to the social studies curriculum. His rationale was that:

> Social-studies instruction should be focused on the goal of developing "good citizens" activated by a personal interest in the common welfare, skilled in social cooperation, and enlightened by insights into the nature and direction of the social process. . . .
>
> The social studies curriculum should emphasize the content, skills, and activities that will direct students toward the goals, values, and behaviors that are an inherited part of a democratic society. Social studies derive their central importance in the school program because of their connection . . . with the elements of social competence in a democratic society.[36]

His proposed scope and sequence is as follows:

Grade	Subject
K	How we do things together
1	Living together
2	Living in our neighborhood
3	Ways of living in other lands
4	Where our ways of living come from
5	Living in the age of machines
6	Richer ways of living
7	The world we live in
8	Our nation's story
9	American communities today

(Curriculum for students of "low" ability)

10	America's basic industries

| 11 | How Americans think |
| 12 | Facing America's future |

(Curriculum for students of "general" ability)

10	Our cultural background
11	American life
12	Trends in American life

(Curriculum for students of "high" ability)

10	Our cultural background
11	Critical forces of modern life
12	Trends in American life

More Recent Recommendations of Social Studies Leaders

The Interdisciplinary or Social Studies Approach. This approach recognizes the limitations of a single discipline and attempts to integrate concepts from several disciplines. The interdisciplinary approach is a relatively old approach, and it has been criticized by some educators who prefer a more academic approach to the separate disciplines. Samuel P. McCutchen promoted this approach early in the 1960s at a time when the separate social sciences were becoming more influential in social studies curriculum development. McCutchen's rationale is as follows:

> One common denominator is the use of interdisciplinary organization of materials at nearly every level. The positive argument for this is that the citizen should bring pertinent information from whatever scholarly discipline to the illumination of civic behavior — it is seldom that only anthropology or economics or history would be sufficient. The negative argument — if it be needed — is that, since there is not space enough in the curriculum for the full dress study of all the components of the scholarly disciplines, interdisciplinary organization seems to be the only feasible way of giving representation to all.[37]

The recommended scope and sequence is:

Grade	Subject
K	Social process at work in the life of the child
1	The family and school in the larger environment

2	The community process with outward manifestations
3	The community process with outward manifestations
4 — 6	The study of cultural areas: Western cultures
7 — 8	Unitary, two-year study of American history
9 — 10	Unitary, two-year study of non-Western cultures
11 — 12	Unitary, two-year study of contemporary problems related to the United States (the problems approach[38]

The Expanding Horizons Approach. This approach is based on the assumption that the curriculum should begin with the experiences of the child. The curriculum then leads the child into the expanded world of school, community, and the nation. While the idea of an expanding horizons curriculum has been written about by many educators, Paul Hanna is usually credited with its design and development. Hanna's rationale is expressed in the following statements:

We begin with the assumption that the nature of the child's capacities for learning are as much a result of previous experiences as they are of genetic factors. . . .

We hold that there is merit in providing all youth first with experiences that help them see the larger warp and woof of the cultural patterns within which they live; we advocate in the beginning school grades the wholistic study of men living in society; we believe that such a beginning makes possible later in the secondary and/or collegiate grades a profitable separation of the several social science and historical threads into special courses for more intensive and meaningful study. . . .[39]

The sequence of themes or emphasis is drawn from the fact that each of us lives within a system or set of expanding communities that starts with the oldest, smallest, and most crucial community — the family placed in the center of the concentric circles — and progresses outward in ever widening bands through the child's neighborhood community; the child's local communities of city, county, and/or metropolis; the state community; the region of states community; the national community.[40]

Hanna's scope and sequence is as follows:

Grade	*Subject*
1	The child's family community; the child's school
2	The child's neighborhood community

3	The child's local communities: city, county, metropolis
4	The child's state community; the child's region-of-states community
5	The United States national community[41]

The Social Science Approach. This approach came into its own in the 1960s, when most social studies curriculum projects emphasized a disciplinary orientation. In 1963 Richard E. Gross and Dwight Allen demonstrated how this approach, among others, could be used in a K-12 curriculum.[42] One premise for this approach rested on the then popular Brunerian idea of teaching the "structure of the discipline." Its roots, however, reach back into the academic traditions of the 19th century. Irving Morrissett and his colleagues at the Social Science Education Consortium promoted the social science approach in the book, *Social Science in the Schools: A Search for Rationale* (1971). Gross and Allen's rationale for the social science approach is that curriculum be based on a "systematic overview of the social sciences by using the disciplines themselves as underlying themes."[43]

A scope and sequence for the social science approach is:

Grade	Subject
1 — 3	Anthropology: used as an introduction to culture — a key to understanding people
4 — 6	Geography: presented as an area-cultures approach that correlates the social sciences
7 — 9	History and sociology: world history taught through a geographic setting, with sociology used to study various social structures
10 — 11	Political science and economics: 10th grade — U.S. history from the beginning to 1876 (political science emphasis) 11th grade — U.S. history from 1876 to the present (economic emphasis)
12	Methodology of various disciplines: electives relating to the disciplines of the social sciences

The Social Roles Approach. In 1978 the SPAN Project (Social Studies/Social Science Education: Priorities, Practices, and Needs) was organized under the direction of Irving Morrissett and his colleagues at the Social Science Education Consortium in Boulder, Colorado. After conducting studies on the background of the social studies and on the current status of the social studies, they developed an experimental curriculum around seven social roles that persons experience during their lifetimes. These roles included: citizen, worker, consumer, family member, friend, member of social groups, and self.[44]

According to the findings of the SPAN Project, the major problem with the social studies is that it "is not organized around or focused on personal and societal goals that help students become effective participants in the social world."[45] The SPAN group's rationale was that the social-role focus could alleviate this problem "by emphasizing the wide range of roles in which people engage — from mainly personal ones such as friend and family member to societal ones such as consumer and citizen."[46]

The SPAN recommended scope and sequence is as follows:

Grade	Social Role
K — 6	Citizen, worker, family, friend, group, self, with each role contributing different topics at each grade level
7	Social studies: focus on self, family, friend, and group
8	U.S history
9	Social studies: focus on worker, consumer, citizen
10	World cultures
11	U.S history
12	U.S government: social science electives

Other Efforts at Defining the Social Studies

From 1958 throughout the 1960s, the National Council for the Social Studies (NCSS) leadership wrestled with the problem of an ill-defined yet ever expanding and more varied social studies curriculum. Ad hoc committee reports,[47] issues of *Social Education*,[48] special bulletins,[49] an abortive National Commission,[50] and eventually a yearbook[51] addressed in one way or another the need for unity and agreement on essentials, which also allowed for some variations and local options. Names of key individuals reappear in many of these publications, in particular: Jack Allen, Howard Anderson, William Cartwright, Dorothy McClure Fraser, Merrill Hartshorn, Erling Hunt, Samuel P. McCutchen, Roy Price, Isadore Starr, L. P. Todd, and Howard Wilson.

The publications of these individuals contained excellent guidelines and suggestions concerning what needed to be accomplished and why. Most, however, gave rather limited attention to the more difficult question of how to implement the guidelines. Once again, a number of alternative scope and sequence patterns were presented. Experimental curriculum centers were suggested to help resolve the conflict arising out of a curriculum developed by experts and the curriculum actually taught by practicing teachers. (The ultimate curriculum is determined by what individual teachers do and don't do in their classrooms!)

It is possible that these NCSS curricular efforts did help bring about the federal sponsorship of several social studies projects in the 1960s, which spawned even more alternatives; but the NCSS was never able to attract the attention, cooperation, and funding necessary for a substantial and protracted effort at national curricular planning. Efforts in this direction seemed almost preordained to failure, because too many individuals, organizations, and institutions just did not communicate with one another or, in many cases, did not even see the need for such mutual action.

The Professionalization of the Social Studies

The professionalization of social studies teachers advanced considerably when a few educators, who were attending a NEA conference in Atlantic City, N.J., in 1921, decided there was a need for a national association for history teachers. The founding group included J. Montgomery Gambrill, Daniel C. Knowlton, Harold Rugg, Earle Rugg, and Roy Hatch. The organization they founded was first called the National Council of Social Studies Teachers.[52] Later the name was changed to the

National Council for the Social Studies (NCSS). Its first president was Albert McKinley, editor of *The Historical Outlook*, which became the temporary voice of the new organization. During this formative period the American Historical Association helped to support the fledgling organization. In the 1930s *The Historical Outlook* became an independent journal and changed its name to *Social Studies*. Then NCSS established *Social Education* as its official journal. Its first editor was Erling Hunt.[53]

Because social studies teachers now had their own organization, they could advance their own professional interests. The council disseminated information to its members and encouraged research in the area of social studies instruction. It also helped to improve the training of social studies teachers and upgraded teacher standards. An annual convention brought teachers together and promoted the exchange of ideas. NCSS and its committees influenced curriculum trends through its reports and its journal, *Social Education*. NCSS also has been a major influence in the professionalization of the social studies field.

Social studies was first the child, then the step-child of the American Historical Association. During the first decades of this century, historians worked closely with high school social studies teachers, but gradually the two groups began to drift apart. Nevertheless, the influence of historians on the social studies curriculum still reflects this early relationship, and old patterns persist in the curriculum today. In recent years more attention has been given to other content areas, especially the social sciences. Although history remained the core discipline of the social studies, by the 1960s it was being pressured to make room for other social science disciplines.

The future direction of the social studies curriculum may well be away from individual disciplines and toward a more integrated approach; but unfortunately, the concept of the social studies, as a clearly defined field in its own right, has not taken root. Some leaders in the field have long argued that the social studies are more than and distinct from history and the social science disciplines. One of the best statements to this point was made in 1962 by Samuel P. McCutchen, former NCSS president.[54] Now, more than 20 years later, we still have not attained a recognized, integrated discipline with an integrity of its own.

The Social Studies Under Attack

Over the years the social studies curriculum has been the target of critics from both within the profession and outside it. Historian Arthur Bestor is an example of an academic critic. In 1953 he attacked the conditions in U.S. education, including the social studies, in his book, *Educational Wasteland: The Retreat from Learning in Our Public Schools.* He was reacting against the changes that had occurred as a result of the progressive movement. In particular, the "life adjustment" curriculum became his target for a wide-ranging attack.

The life adjustment approach in the late 1940s was an attempt to build a pupil-centered curriculum based on the needs of the child and not on the concepts of a discipline. It was an outgrowth of the child-centered approach introduced by the progressives in the early 20th century.[55] In practice, the life adjustment curriculum had only moderate success and was adopted by only a few schools, but it served as a convenient staw man for Bestor's attacks.

The "traditionalists" opposed the life adjustment approach. They believed that the curriculum should be based on the content of the disciplines and not on the child's needs. From their perspective, the child was to be trained in the disciplines. Bestor charged that the school curriculum was void of the intellectual content that was needed for our national survival. Cold War fear was at a high pitch at this time.

Bestor's specific attacks on the social studies focused on their interdisciplinary nature. According to him, the watered-down social studies content neglected the serious study of history and the social sciences. In place of social studies he advocated a disciplinary approach in which history and the social sciences would be taught as separate courses.[56] Bestor offered a plan for revitalizing the curriculum. He did not intend to destroy the public schools, but to reform them. In 1956 he and a group of like-minded individuals founded the Council for Basic Education, an organization that lobbied for reorganization of the curriculum along rigorous academic lines and with an emphasis on teaching basic skills. The current back-to-basics movement in education reflects many of the views Arthur Bestor would have endorsed.

Over the years, other critics have had an influence on the direction and nature of the social studies curriculum. Reform movements competed with traditional approaches to produce further changes in the social studies curriculum.

The "New Social Studies" 1957-1975

When World War II ended, the United States was in a position of world leadership; the wartime economy was converted to peacetime production. European nations had to rebuild their economic systems, and Germany was an occupied and divided nation. The Cold War between the United States and the Soviet Union led to competition in atomic weapons and space technology.

In October 1957, the Soviet Union successfully launched the first orbiting earth satellite, called "Sputnik." American reaction was one of surprise and dismay. The American public had been told that their nation would be the first to orbit such a satellite because the Soviet Union was not considered a technically advanced nation at this time. Militarily, this meant that the nation was no longer protected by the Atlantic or the Pacific Oceans, which historically had served as natural barriers.

When Congress investigated the reasons for the Soviet technological advances and invited Admiral Hyman Rickover, father of the atomic submarine, to testify, he blamed American education for failing to produce qualified scientists to meet the Soviet challenge. Rickover was especially critical of the progressive education programs that remained popular among some educators in the 1940s and 1950s. He claimed that while the Soviet Union was educating large numbers of engineers, mathematicians, and scientists, American educators were involved with life adjustment education, vocational training, and other programs that did not stress scientific disciplines.

After considering several issues pertaining to education, Congress enacted legislation aimed at reforming and revitalizing mathematics and science programs. Private funds also became available for the development of educational programs. Although science and mathematics were the priority curriculum areas for reform, there was a receptive mood in the country for innovation in other curriculum areas.

In September 1959, the National Academy of Science sponsored a meeting of scholars at Woods Hole, Mass. These scholars were asked to make recommendations pertaining to the teaching of math and science in the public schools. Jerome S. Bruner, a Harvard psychologist, attended this meeting and summarized his views and the views of others in the book, *The Process of Education*. This little book was to become highly influential in the curriculum reform movement that was about to begin. In this book Bruner recommended that the new curricula emphasize four fundamental principles: the structure of the discipline, readiness to learn, intuitive and analytical thinking, and motivation — all of which Bruner considered important in the learning process. Many of the new social studies curriculum projects followed these principles to some extent, and the materials developed for these projects contained several common characteristics. One characteristic was the inquiry method of teaching in which the student is expected to perform problem-solving and decision-making tasks utilizing critical thinking. It is interesting to note that this approach is one that was acceptable to progressive educators.

The federal government also funded evaluation and dissemination projects, such as those of the Social Science Education Consortium in Boulder, Colorado. The consortium became the ERIC/CHESS national clearinghouse for research and programs in the social studies and the social sciences, where all types of documents and information pertaining to the teaching of the social studies are indexed and made available to teachers throughout the country.

These decades will be remembered by educators as a time of great experimentation and innovation. There were about 100 projects in the social studies area alone. Some were disciplinary, others multi- or interdisciplinary. Some were directed at a single grade level, others at several grades or across the entire K-12 curriculum. Several had short-term popularity and influence; few had long-term holding power. But they provided teachers with a cafeteria of curricular selections never before available. Unfortunately, this "do-your-own-thing" era contributed to an increasing balkanization of the social studies curriculum.

The Growing Influence of Social Sciences in the "New Social Studies"

The "new social studies" tended to emphasize the role of the social sciences. While not all educators favored this approach, some of the leaders in the social studies field in the 1960s were willing to explore this approach in such academically oriented curriculum development efforts as the High School Geography Project and the Sociological Resources for Secondary Schools project.

Other educators were interested in the various methodological approaches of social science as a new direction for the social studies. For example, Stanley Wronski recommended that curriculum development focus on the tools and methods of the social scientist in order to generate new topics, interpretations, research, and knowledge for the social studies.[57] Economist Lawrence Senesh recommended what he called the "orchestration" of the social sciences into a social studies curriculum, drawing on each discipline at an appropriate time. Senesh himself developed an elementary program with an economics perspective. Byron Massialas and C. Benjamin Cox recommended a social science approach as a means of dealing with social knowledge. According to them, knowledge could be used as a way of focusing on persistent social problems of American society.[58] By 1965, when more than 500 school districts were contacted by the NCSS regarding curriculum development, almost all reported some curriculum revision work, and the social sciences had become an important emphasis in their curriculum work.[59]

The Emphasis on Values in the "New Social Studies"

While the social sciences received great attention during the "new social studies" movement, some educators recommended a values approach to societal problems for the social studies. Shirley Engle was one who advocated the societal problems approach. This perspective for curriculum planning places high priority on values and value problems which exist in the society, with the structure of the discipline playing a significant but supportive role.[60]

Maurice Hunt and Lawrence Metcalf recommended the study of social problems as the central theme of the social studies curriculum. They believed that "the foremost aim of instruction in high school is to help students examine issues reflectively in the closed areas of American culture."[61] Fred Newmann, Donald Oliver, and James Shaver developed a curriculum approach based on social issues in American society in their book, *Teaching Public Issues in the High School.*

During the 1970s differences emerged between academicians and social studies educators. In 1979 Irving Morrissett addressed these differences in an article in which he attempted to defend the academicians' approach to the curriculum.[62] However, during the 1970s the social studies curriculum moved away from some of the themes of the "new social studies" movement. The pendulum of curricular thinking and change was swinging backward. By the 1980s numerous social studies teachers were beginning to have doubts about the work done in the era of the "new social studies." Older perspectives such as an emphasis on citizenship education began to reappear. At present there is a strong sense of uneasiness over the social studies·curriculum and the future directions that it should take.

The social studies were inundated by an expanding cafeteria of competing choices from the social studies projects of the 1960s. In an era of "anything goes, everything is equal" relativism in American society in the late 1960s and early 1970s, the schools offered mini-courses, electives, experimental options, and independent study arrangements that further affected traditional curricular courses.

The curriculum also faced a new wave of demands calling for ethnic studies, values education, law-related education, global studies, women's studies, free-enterprise schooling, and career preparation, to name a few. Probably the stability that was maintained was due to entrenched, noninnovative teachers and to the conventional textbooks from the major publishing houses.

As Vietnam, the youth revolt, and Watergate faded into the past, and as demands for standards, quality, accountability, and back-to-basics became the major items on the public's education agenda, the social studies tended to be overlooked and even discounted. That the field has survived may be more the result of the inertia of the traditional social studies curriculum and the public outcry for more citizenship education than as a result of any united action by social studies leaders. At this juncture the situation is not just muddled; it is quite desperate, calling for creative and energetic action by those of us concerned not only over the future of the social studies field but about the future of this society.

The Need for a National Scope and Sequence Framework in the Social Studies

Scope and sequence is the technical aspect of curriculum development. Through this process, subject matter, approaches, and learning activities are organized for instructional purposes. This process may be done at different levels, from the national to that of the individual school. Historically, national committees recommended and developed scope and sequence patterns for K-12. Leaders in the social studies also have recommended scope and sequence patterns that emphasize a particular perspective. Textbook publishers have developed series of textbooks based on a scope and sequence pattern. In more recent times school districts have developed scope and sequence patterns and published them in local curriculum guides. State departments of education also have developed scope and sequence patterns that are contained in state guides and "frameworks." These state guides are important because frequently they are used as the basis for statewide textbook adoptions.

To those of us committed to the idea of a national framework for the social studies — even with certain options and variations — one of the greatest challenges facing us is the fact that ultimate control of the curriculum rests with 50 different states. In some manner the Americanization of America — the growing likenesses that stretch from coast to coast and our ever more common needs — has to be recognized by state legislatures so that state departments of education are allowed to cooperate in the development of a national framework for the social studies.

Curriculum change will occur when scope and sequence patterns change, but that is but one part of a total long-term effort if substantial changes are to take place in classrooms. Developing a timely scope and sequence is as much a political activity as it is an educational one. It involves a series of compromises resulting from the input of academicians, consultants, special interest groups, and various committees, each with a different agenda. Furthermore, today's teachers are not willing to let others do this important work for them. Given the broad and confused field of the social studies, it seems clear that some central body, such as the National Council for the Social Studies, must take on as a prime responsibility a number of the tasks of scope and sequence development.

Components of a Timely Scope and Sequence

The development of a timely scope and sequence involves a process that includes the following components:

1. *Developing a Rationale*. A rationale includes a perspective on society and on how children learn. The rationale sets forth how these perspectives will be emphasized throughout the curriculum.

2. *Establishing a Social Studies Approach*. The rationale is used as the basis for a social studies approach that helps the curriculum developer identify specific educational goals for the curriculum. In 1982 Dynneson and Gross identified eight possible different approaches.[63]

3. *Identifying Educational Objectives*. Educational objectives serve as the general guidelines for the curriculum. Educational objectives provide the criteria that are used for selecting topics, content, and instructional materials. These same objectives are used in the evaluation process.

4. *Identifying Key Instructional Concepts and Competencies*. The identification of specific concepts and skills is an essential part of scope and sequence development. This component includes provisions for repeating and reinforcing these concepts and skills at increasing levels of sophistication.

5. *Developing Courses and Units*. This component requires the efforts of many classroom teachers, who develop the courses and units

that have been established in the scope and sequence. This component involves more direct input from teachers than do the other tasks identified in this process.

6. *Pilot Testing the Curriculum.* Piloting or field testing involves teaching the courses and units experimentally to representative groups of students. Through this procedure, defective aspects of the curriculum can be identified and changes made prior to implementing the new curriculum.

7. *Implementing the New Curriculum Program.* Once adopted, the new curriculum is taught as the regular social studies program to all students. Intensive dissemination activities, inservice retraining, and supervisory reinforcement are all essential if the implementation process is to be effective.

8. *Evaluating the Curriculum.* New curriculum programs should be evaluated on a continuing basis and at each grade level. The criteria for this evaluation are based on the rationale and the course objectives.

Curriculum Adoption

When school districts make changes in their social studies curriculum, these changes either evolve slowly over time or they are rapid because of imposed new state regulations. For example, the California State Board of Education recently adopted a new social studies framework as a basis for new text adoptions, which leads local school districts to alter their existing social studies programs. One such alteration returns, after many years, the teaching of government and civics to the 9th grade from the 12th. Such changes pose many problems, ranging from entrenched habits of teachers to the selection of new learning materials at proper reading levels. Such alterations in sequence are difficult to implement, but in California extensive implementation activities are going on throughout the state to help bring about acceptance of the new curriculum.

Other states are involved with implementation plans for new statewide programs in the social studies. The Texas Education Agency recently asked local districts and areas to make recommendations for revised state requirements. This effort encompasses a two-year program of planning, informing, and action. The state of Maryland is just completing a complex process of scope and sequence revision. The successes and difficulties encountered in such efforts need to be publicized and shared.

Even a single change in a scope and sequence calls for a carefully planned implementation process. It does no good, for example, to issue an edict replacing a program of social studies electives at the senior high level with a required core of courses. Such a change calls for a well-planned, lengthy, and detailed process of implementation. This transitional phase between curriculum development and curriculum adoption is a crucial one, which determines the success or failure of numerous curriculum development programs. During this phase, teacher orientation is critical. Unless teachers understand and agree with the changes, implementation simply will not take place. The proof of any curriculum change is only on the firing line.

Implementing curriculum change involves human relationships. Hilda Taba acknowledged the crucial importance of such relationships when she wrote: "An effective strategy of curriculum change must proceed on a double agenda, working simultaneously to change ideas about curriculum and to change human dynamics."[64] Therefore, the implementation process must include means for the modification of attitudes. In addition, positive experiences need to be built into the change process. Teachers who are asked to execute changes should be given opportunities to observe other mentors successfully involved in revised courses. Further, they need opportunities to examine alternatives, to question cherished ideas, and to assess the effects of the change. Mandated changes that do not allow for expression of these concerns could lead to negative feelings that will affect the implementation of a new program. Changes that do not involve the classroom teacher — from initial needs assessment to final evaluations — will ultimately fail. There must be specific strategies designed to win the support of the classroom teacher.

There is not space in this fastback to detail the process of curricular change. A bulletin of the National Council for the Social Studies, *Social Studies Curriculum Improvement*, reports several illustrative case studies.[65] Three approaches by which curriculum changes are attempted are the imposed or mandated curriculum, the derived curriculum, and the jointly planned curriculum.

The imposed curriculum originates from outside local school districts. It often is introduced by a state education agency. For instance, the state department of education may have to execute curriculum change as a result of laws passed by the state legislature. Because of the authority of the state, the local school district must adopt the new program. Teachers may not have participated in the development of the new curriculum, but they are the key to successful execution of the program. Therefore, the imposed curriculum should allow for some degree of local participation in order to relieve tensions and resentments and to achieve the support of the classroom teacher.

The derived curriculum is one that originates within the local school district. It is planned, developed, and implemented by the local classroom teachers. The process of developing a derived curriculum was described earlier under "Components of a Timely Scope and Sequence." Because those who are to execute the new curriculum have participated in its development, they have become convinced, in most cases, that the new curriculum has several advantages over existing programs. Therefore, change is less difficult because many obstacles have been overcome during the curriculum development process.

The jointly planned curriculum may originate outside the local school district; however, the details of the program may be left to each local school district. Local school officials and classroom teachers have some options to modify this curriculum. For example, a national committee may present a new social studies curriculum and prescribe a broad framework of topics and/or specific courses, but the local school district is expected to develop detailed offerings in the form of course units. Some options and electives may be left entirely to local decision. Teachers can be involved in the work of curriculum committees that develop course units within the new curriculum. The new curriculum might also be pilot tested in local school districts. The result of the pilot tests would determine the final form of the new curriculum. Eventually some plan of cooperative evaluation between a national commission, the state, and county and city districts could be instituted.

These three approaches to curriculum changes differ in terms of teachers' roles and responsibilities. Teachers tend to support curriculum changes that meet their perceived needs, that work with pupils, and that allow them to participate in both developmental and implementation processes. Nevertheless, teachers frequently complain about the lack of specificity in the frameworks provided them. They also normally do not have the time and facilities, let alone a commitment, to review and revamp the conventional courses they have been teaching for some time. They find it even more difficult to develop entirely new offerings from bare guidelines. The implications are clear for those who are desirous for timely and thorough evolution of a new scope and sequence for the social studies.

Next Steps in
Scope and Sequence Development

Twenty years ago Richard Gross and Dwight Allen presented a detailed plan for a national restructuring of the social studies curriculum.[66] Their call for a clearinghouse of information has taken place with the establishment of the ERIC center for the social studies. But their major recommendations for the establishment of a national research center in social studies education and for a national commission to sponsor and organize the development and pilot testing of several alternative scope and sequence designs have never taken hold.

Currently, what is needed is a massive, cooperatively mounted plan for scope and sequence revision at the national level. Representatives of state departments of education, large school districts, related academic organizations, key public/lay groups, teacher educators, and appropriate education associations need to be drawn together in this crucial activity. The National Council for the Social Studies could serve as the convenor of such a group. Its work would have to have a substantial financing from several sources. It would also require adequate time for deliberations including a number of extended joint meetings. This body could be designated the National Commission for Social Studies Organization. Its responsibilities would be to develop a rationale, set goals, and develop criteria for content selection and placement. It would oversee the work of the National Social Studies Task Force and its various subcommittees. It would cooperate with the National Social Studies Task Force in establishing the plans and parameters for the evolution, piloting, and assessment of the model, experimental social studies K-12 curriculum. Ultimately it would be responsible for forwarding the findings and recommendations that accrue from the efforts of the National Social Studies Task Force and its committees.

Some members of the foregoing commission, augmented by a number of specialists appointed by the commission, would constitute the National Social Studies Task Force. The task force could be organized into working parties on a regional basis. This will facilitate continuing communication as these working parties develop the details of the scope and sequence option for which they are responsible. These working parties would, of course, seek needed help and feedback from local school districts as they evolve the recommended program to be tested in their region. Chairpersons of these working parties should probably be members of the national commission, thus ensuring exchange of information. The working parties would cooperate in the identification of key concepts and generalizations to be emphasized across and within each scope and sequence. They may also agree on the prime skills to be emphasized; but the design for organizing these skills may vary, depending on the particular structure of different K-12 programs.

Important subsequent steps for local planning, inservice education, and continuing review and assessment would have to be developed cooperatively by the national commission and the task force regional committees with state departments of education and participating school districts. The details of the cooperative efforts need not be outlined here, but it should be recognized that such a large-scale development and research program is going to take at least five to ten years, depending on the overall design and the manner in which school districts are involved in the regional piloting.

We realize that there are many arguments against and roadblocks to what we have proposed. But how much longer can we condone the current unfortunate conditions in the social studies field? Cannot committed and reasonable leaders finally evolve a timely scope and sequence for the social studies that incorporates 1) the systematic study of key knowledge and related skills, 2) the personal development of students, and 3) the growth of socio/civic concern and participation? Our challenge is to shape a program of social studies education that will preserve the worthy elements of our culture and at the same time enable young citizens to promote, meet, and control change. We must solve the paradox of our field — one that has to balance cultural commitment with the means and ends of social progress.

Footnotes

1. At this writing the published report of the conference held at Racine, Wisconsin, in August 1982 was not as yet available.
2. Richard E. Gross, "The Status of the Social Studies in the Public Schools of the United States," *Social Education* 41 (March 1977): 194-200.
3. Douglas P. Superka, Sharryl Hawke, and Irving Morrissett, "The Current and Future Status of the Social Studies," *Social Education* 44 (May 1980): 362-69.
4. Richard E. Gross and Thomas L. Dynneson, "Regenerating the Social Studies from Old Dirges to New Directions," *Social Education* 44 (May 1980): 370-74.
5. Irving Morrissett, Sharryl Hawke, and Douglas P. Superka, "Six Problems for Social Studies in the 1980s," *Social Education* 44 (Nov./Dec. 1980): 561-69.
6. Richard E. Gross and Dwight Allen, "Time for a National Effort to Develop the Social Studies Curriculum" *Phi Delta Kappan*, May 1963, pp. 360-66.
7. R. Murray Thomas and Dale L. Brubaker, *Curriculum Patterns in Elementary Social Studies* (Belmont, Calif.: Wadsworth Publishing Company, 1971).
8. Freeman R. Butts, "Historical Perspective on Civic Education in the United States," in *Education for Responsible Citizenship*, ed. B. Frank Brown (New York: McGraw-Hill Company, 1977), p. 47.
9. Ibid.
10. Gary Wehlage and Eugene M. Anderson, *Social Studies Curriculum in Perspective* (Englewood Cliffs, N.J.: Prentice Hall, 1972), p. 3.
11. Butts, *"Historical Perspectives,"* p. 56.
12. Earle U. Rugg, "A Teacher — Pupil Program in Citizenship Education," in *The Future of the Social Studies*, ed. James A. Michener (Washington, D.C.: National Council for the Social Studies, 1939), p. 127.
13. Ibid.
14. Butts, "Historical Perspectives," p. 57.
15. Jack Allen, "Assessing Recent Developments in the Social Studies," *Social Education* 31 (February, 1967): 99-100.
16. Butts, "Historical Perspectives", p. 57.
17. Hazel W. Hertzberg, *Social Studies Reform 1880 — 1980*, A SPAN Report (Boulder, Colo.: Social Science Education Consortium, Inc., 1981), p. 27.
18. Ibid., p. 25.
19. Ibid., pp. 28-29.
20. Ibid., p. 4.

21. Peter A. Soderberg, "Charles A. Beard and the Commission on the Social Studies 1929-1933: A Reappraisal," *Social Education* 31 (October 1967): 465.
22. Butts, "Historical Perspectives", pp. 61, 62.
23. Ibid., p. 61.
24. Hertzberg, *Social Studies Reform*, p. 45.
25. Ibid., p. 52.
26. Mary G. Kelty, "Principles, Procedures, and Content," in *The Future of the Social Studies*, ed. James A. Michener (Washington, D.C.: National Council for the Social Studies, 1939), p. 60.
27. Samuel P. McCutchen, "Comments on a Social-Studies Program," in *The Future of the Social Studies*, ed. James A. Michener (Washington, D.C.: National Council for the Social Studies, 1939), pp. 83, 84.
28. Ibid., p. 86.
29. Ibid., pp. 88-90.
30. Frances Morehouse, "A Course of Social Studies for American Public Schools," in *The Future of the Social Studies*, ed. James A. Michener (Washington, D.C.: National Council for the Social Studies, 1939), p. 107.
31. Ibid.
32. Harold Rugg, "Curriculum Design in the Social Studies: What I Believe," in *The Future of the Social Studies*, ed. James A. Michener (Washington, D.C.: National Council for the Social Studies, 1939), p. 141.
33. Ibid.
34. Ibid., pp. 143-147.
35. Donnal V. Smith, "What Shall We Teach in Social Studies," in *The Future of the Social Studies*, ed. James A. Michener (Washington, D.C.: National Council for the Social Studies, 1939), p. 160.
36. Howard E. Wilson, "A Social-Studies Course of Study," in *The Future of the Social Studies*, ed. James A. Michener, (Washington, D.C.: National Council for the Social Studies, 1939), p. 168.
37. Samuel P. McCutchen, "A Proposed Grade Placement for the Social Studies," in *The Social Studies and the National Interest*, ad hoc Committee Report (Washington, D.C.: National Council for the Social Studies, November, 1962), p. 17.
38. Ibid., pp. 18, 19.
39. Paul R. Hanna, "Revising the Social Studies: What Is Needed?" *Social Education* 27 (April 1963): 191.
40. Ibid., p. 192.
41. Ibid., p. 193.
42. Gross and Allen, "Time for a National Effort," pp. 360-365.
43. Ibid., p. 364.
44. Douglas P. Superka and Sharryl Hawke, "Social Roles: A Focus for Social Studies in the 1980s," *Social Education* 44 (Nov./Dec. 1980): 577-86.

45. Douglas P. Superka and Sharryl Hawke, *Social Roles: A Focus for Social Studies in the 1980s*, Project SPAN (Boulder, Colo.: Social Science Education Consortium, 1982), p. 18.

46. Ibid.

47. National Council for the Social Studies, "The Social Studies and the National Interest," ad hoc Committee Report, mimeographed (Washington, D.C.: NCSS, November 1962).

48. See, for example, *Special Issue on Revising the Social Studies, Social Education* (April 1963).

49. Dorothy McClure Fraser and Samuel P. McCutchen, eds. *Social Studies in Transition: Guidelines for Change*, Curriculum Series #12, mimeographed (Washington, D.C.: National Council for the Social Studies, 1965).

50. National Commission on the Social Studies, "Curriculum Planning in American Schools: The Social Studies," Howard E. Wilson, Chairman, mimeographed draft report (Washington, D.C.: NCSS, November 1958).

51. Dorothy McClure Fraser, ed., *Social Studies Curriculum Development: Prospects and Problems*, 39th Yearbook (Washington, D.C.: National Council for the Social Studies, 1969).

52. Louis M. Vanaria, "The National Council for the Social Studies: A Voluntary Organization for Professional Service," *Social Education* 35 (November 1970): 782-86, 795.

53. Hertzberg, *Social Studies Reform*, p. 5.

54. Samuel P. McCutchen, "A Discipline for the Social Studies," *Social Education* 27 (February 1963): 61-65. He included four elements: the societal goals of America, the heritage and values of Western civilization, the dimensions and interrelationships of today's world, and a specific process of rational inquiry and the tenets of good scholarship.

55. Wehlage, *Social Studies Curriculum*, p. 5.

56. Arthur Bestor, *The Restoration of Learning: A Program for Redeeming the Unfulfilled Promise of American Education* (New York: Alfred A. Knopf, 1956), pp. 126-29.

57. Stanley P. Wronski, "A Proposed Breakthrough in the Social Studies," *Social Education* 23 (May 1959): 215-18.

58. Byron Massialas and C. Benjamin Cox, *Inquiry in Social Studies* (New York: McGraw-Hill, 1966), p. 53.

59. Jack Allen, "Recent Developments," pp. 99-103.

60. Fred R. Smith and C. Benjamin Cox, *New Strategies and Curriculum in Social Studies* (Chicago: Rand McNally and Company, 1969).

61. Maurice P. Hunt and Lawrence C. Metcalf, *Teaching High School Social Studies* (New York: Harper and Row, 1968).

62. Irving Morrissett, "Citizenship, Social Studies, and the Academician," *Social Education* 43 (January 1979): 12-17.

63. Thomas L. Dynneson and Richard E. Gross, "Citizenship Education and the Social Studies: Which Is Which?" *The Social Studies* 73 (Sept./Oct. 1982): 229-35.

64. Hilda Taba, *Curriculum Development: Theory and Practice* (New York: Harcourt, Brace and World, 1962), p. 455.

65. Raymond H. Muessig, ed., *Social Studies Curriculum Improvement*, National Council for the Social Studies Bulletin 55 (Washington, D.C. 1978). See also Craig Kissock, *Curriculum Planning for Social Studies Teaching* (New York: John Wiley and Sons, 1981). The issues surrounding content change and placement are also addressed by Wayne L. Herman, Jr., "What Should Be Taught Where?" *Social Education* 47 (February 1983): 94-100; and by Gerald Ponder, "Getting Real: Suggestions for Revising the Social Studies Curriculum," *Educational Leadership* 40 (January 1983): 56-61.

66. Gross and Allen, "Time for a National Effort," pp. 360-65.